EXPLORE THE WORLD

EARTH SCIENCE

On the Arctic Tundra

TRINA LAWRENCE

TABLE OF CONTENTS

What Is the Arctic Tundra? 2
Where Is the Arctic Tundra? 4
Tundra Plant Life 5
Tundra Animals 8
Insects on the Tundra 16
Glossary/Index 20

PIONEER VALLEY EDUCATIONAL PRESS, INC

WHAT IS THE ARCTIC TUNDRA?

In the far north,
there is a very cold place
called the Arctic tundra.

The tundra is a place where
the winters are long and cold
and the summers are short and cool.

3

WHERE IS THE ARCTIC TUNDRA?

ARCTIC CIRCLE   NORTH POLE

The Arctic tundra is found around the North Pole.

In the winter, the tundra is in the dark almost all day.
In the summer, the sun shines all day and almost all night.

summer
Arctic Circle

winter
Arctic Circle

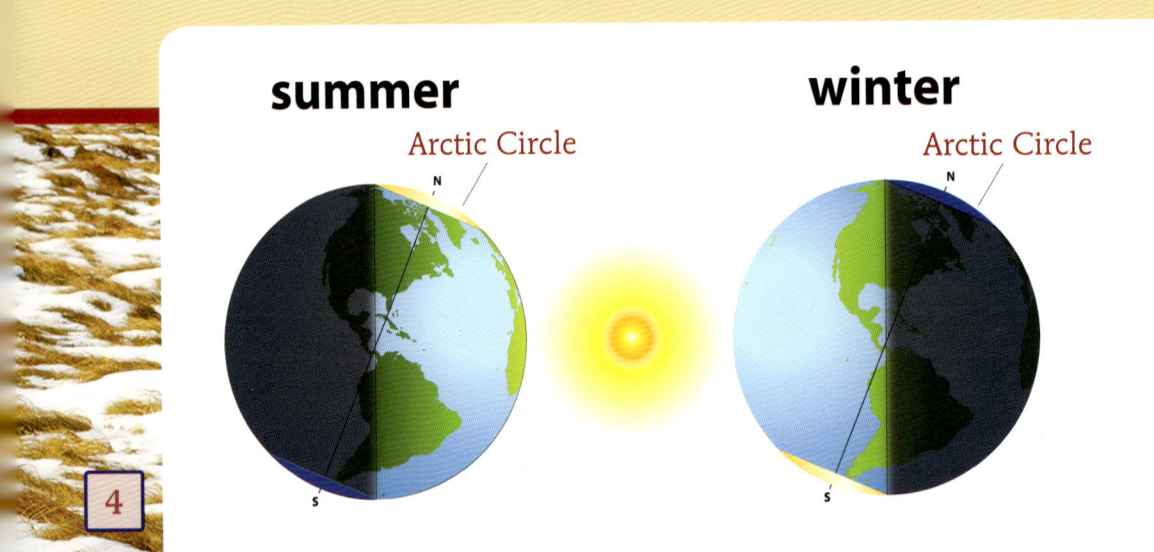

TUNDRA PLANT LIFE

Tall trees do not grow on the tundra. The only plants that grow on the tundra are small bushes that can live where it is very cold. They grow close to the ground where they can stay out of the wind.

MORE TO EXPLORE

BEARBERRY is one kind of plant that grows on the tundra. The plant has small red berries that bears like to eat. That is where it gets its name.

In winter, the tundra is white with snow and ice.

In summer, the tundra is very colorful.

The ground is covered with pink, purple, and yellow flowers.

Here is an **ARCTIC POPPY**. It is a beautiful flower that grows on the tundra. The flower moves to follow the heat of the sun.

7

TUNDRA ANIMALS

Some animals live all year on the tundra.

Other animals live on the tundra only in summer.

In winter, the animals travel south, so they can be where it is warmer.

MORE TO EXPLORE

Here is an **ARCTIC FOX**. It lives on the tundra. It is about the size of a house cat. It has a long, bushy tail that it uses to wrap around itself like a blanket.

Animals that live all year on the tundra will eat a lot in the fall to make a **layer** of fat called **blubber**. They also grow a thick coat of fur for winter. This helps keep them warm all winter.

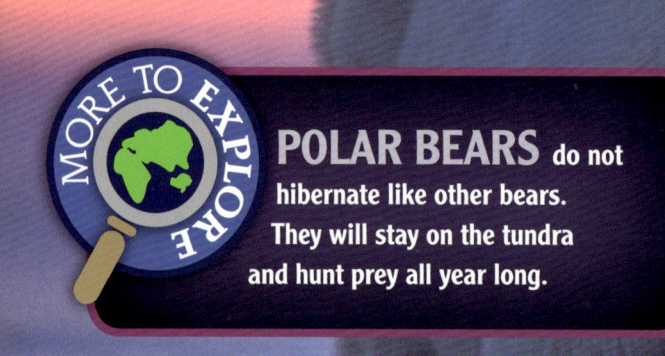

MORE TO EXPLORE

POLAR BEARS do not hibernate like other bears. They will stay on the tundra and hunt prey all year long.

ANIMALS THAT LIVE YEAR-ROUND ON THE TUNDRA

- arctic hare
- arctic fox
- musk ox
- weasel
- wolf
- caribou
- polar bear
- snowy owl

In the winter, some animals grow a white winter coat of fur or feathers.

They **blend** into the white snow. This makes it hard for other animals to see them.

The **ARCTIC HARE** lives on the tundra. It has a blue-gray coat in the summer that turns to a bright white in the winter.

13

In the spring, many animals move to the tundra. They come a long way to eat the tundra plants and have babies.

MORE TO EXPLORE

Some **CARIBOU** live all year on the tundra and others visit just in the summer. Caribou babies are born on the tundra in the early summer.

MORE TO EXPLORE

The **TUNDRA SWAN** flies north to the tundra in the spring. Tundra swans build nests near pools or lakes. They lay four or five eggs. The eggs hatch in the early summer.

INSECTS ON THE TUNDRA

Insects and spiders live on the tundra, too. The insects **hatch** and grow in the spring and summer. At the end of the summer, they lay eggs that will hatch the next spring.

INSECTS THAT LIVE ON THE TUNDRA

- mosquito
- blowfly
- beetle
- arctic bumblebee
- swallowtail butterfly
- brush-footed butterfly
- flea

The Arctic tundra is a cold and windy place, but it is home for many beautiful plants and interesting animals.

CYCLE OF LIFE ON THE TUNDRA

01 Small animals eat plants.

02 The plant-eating animals are hunted by small meat-eating animals.

03 The smaller animals are hunted and eaten by larger meat-eating animals.

04 When the animals die, their remains are broken down by insects and spiders. This helps the soil and plants to grow.

GLOSSARY

blend
to mix together

blubber
the fat on polar bears and whales and other animals that live in the water

hatch
come out of an egg

layer
a part that lies over or under another

North Pole
the most northern part of the Earth

INDEX

animals 8–9, 10–11, 18
arctic fox 9, 11
arctic hare 11, 12
arctic poppy 6
blend 12
blubber 10
caribou 11, 14
flowers 6
hatch 15
insects 16–17
layer 10
North Pole 4
plants 5, 18
polar bears 10–11
spring 14, 16
summer 6, 16
tundra swan 15
winter 2, 4, 6, 8, 10, 12